© **Sunshine of Happiness**
BY SANDEEP RAVIDUTT SHARMA

Table of Contents

Foreword IV

Sunshine of happiness...1

© **Sunshine of Happiness**
BY SANDEEP RAVIDUTT SHARMA

Foreword

This book provides you with a list of 100 quotes and thoughts about LIFE, churned out by my mind with the consciousness, grace and energy of Shiva Shakti. I'm sure if you keep reading, referring, sharing these thoughts and quotes about LIFE, you may derive inspiration and develop good understanding of various perspectives and facts. Explore the Sunshine of happiness within. You don't need to go places fo find peace and happiness, it's right in your heart and mind.

"Attract happiness through appreciating what you have rather than cribbing for what you could not get. Happiness multiplies when your kindness brings a smile on the face of the other."

I sincerely hope, you will find this book amazing, interesting, rejuvenating, unique and a constant source of Inspiration.

Thank You and Happy Reading.

© **Sunshine of Happiness**
BY SANDEEP RAVIDUTT SHARMA

© Copyright 2018 Sandeep Ravidutt Sharma - All rights reserved.

In no way is it legal to reproduce, duplicate, or transmit any part of this document in either electronic means or in printed format. Recording of this publication is strictly prohibited and any storage of this document is not allowed unless with written permission from the publisher. All rights reserved. The information provided herein is stated to be truthful and consistent, in that any liability, in terms of inattention or otherwise, by any usage or abuse of any policies, processes, or directions contained within is the solitary and utter responsibility of the recipient reader. Under no circumstances will any legal responsibility or blame be held against the author / publisher for any reparation, damages, or monetary loss due to the information herein, either directly or indirectly. The author own all copyrights.

Legal Notice:
This book is copyright protected. This is only for personal use. You cannot amend, distribute, sell, use, quote or paraphrase any part or the content within this book without the consent of the author or copyright owner. Legal action will be pursued if this is breached.

Disclaimer Notice:
Please note the information contained within this book is for motivational, educational and knowledge sharing purpose only. Every attempt has been made to provide the reader accurate, up to date and reliable complete information. No warranties of any kind are expressed or implied. Readers acknowledge that the author is not engaging in the rendering of legal, financial, medical or professional advice. By reading this document, the reader agrees that under no circumstances the author / publisher is responsible for any losses, direct or indirect, which are incurred as a result of the use of information contained within this document, including, but not limited to errors, omissions, or inaccuracies.

If you have further questions, contact on **Tel: +919969256731**
Email: sandeepraviduttsharma@gmail.com

© **Sunshine of Happiness**
BY SANDEEP RAVIDUTT SHARMA

Dedication

This book is dedicated to **Shiva Shakti** - the epitome of love. Lord Shiva is pure consciousness symbolising the masculine principle. Goddess Shakti symbolises the active feminine energy of Shiva and is synonymously identified with **Tripura Sundari, Sati** or **Parvati**.

These primal principles are also called as PURUSHA representing consciousness and PRAKRITI denoting the nature. Shiva and Shakti are manifestations of the all-in-one divine consciousness. Shiva is the paternal love of God that gives us consciousness, knowledge and clarity. Shakti is the motherly love of God that showers warmth, care and ensures our protection. Shiva and Shakti exist within each of us as the masculine and feminine energy.

To please **Shiva Shakti** praying for the well being, love, happiness, strength, positive energy and success of my readers in their life, I hereby recite the following mantra...

"Sarva Mangala Mangalye Shive Sarvartha Sadhike Sharanye Tryambake Gauri Narayani Namostute"

© **Sunshine of Happiness**
BY SANDEEP RAVIDUTT SHARMA

Photo Credits

The beautiful and amazing photograph used for the book cover is clicked by **Anne Marie** from **Norway**.

You can visit her excellent photo gallery at **Instagram: @millymollymandy**

Sunshine of Happiness

© **Sunshine of Happiness**
BY SANDEEP RAVIDUTT SHARMA

Positivity introduces you to the Sunshine of happiness.

© **Sunshine of Happiness**
BY SANDEEP RAVIDUTT SHARMA

Dark clouds introduce rains to the world with thunder. Rains provide breath of life. Love dark clouds and rains alike.

Winners create and not imitate.

© **Sunshine of Happiness**
BY SANDEEP RAVIDUTT SHARMA

Don't run away from life challenges. Face them. Move towards positivity, and find the right company among people who can motivate. Remind your own self again and again that you can fight it out. Live in the present.

The universe is constantly expanding, so are our thoughts. When good thoughts start dominating your day to day action, it's a signal that you are on the right path and would soon meet success.

Avoid quick decision if you are not satisfied or doubt the outcome of the proposed activity. Decide quickly when it's matter of life and death.

When you walk straight in life, nobody can stop you from winning.

When peace prevails at all ends, it's a matter of silent celebration.

Keep smiling not to conquer the world but to conquer the hearts.

Remember God at all times.

Understanding the world becomes easy if you have understood own self.

When nothing works trust in the Lord still works.

When you trust someone, then, only expect trust from others. Trust is mutual.

Keep trying, and Success would befriend you some day.

Treat failure as experience gained.

Unless you have decided to do something in life, how would anyone know and support you in your mission?

Real friends are those who accept you the way you are.

Take a vow to achieve and not abandon.

Attract abundance through positive thinking.

© **Sunshine of Happiness**
BY SANDEEP RAVIDUTT SHARMA

When you walk on the staircase, it is advisable to take one step at a time. Those who skip some stairs in a hurry run the risk of getting hurt.

Sunshine of Happiness
BY SANDEEP RAVIDUTT SHARMA

Take it easy... We are here to live our life and not to solve some mathematical equation. Take a deep breath. Live in the present. Do things which make you happy. Share your happiness with people who understands you or are making attempt to understand. Forgot the past if it is not worth remembering. Focus on your strengths, work on your weaknesses. Keep a positive frame of mind. Don't think too much...think only of the present moment. Try to improve your visualization...draw in your mind with inputs from your heart your desired world. Sooner or later. You will see it live. Take it easy...

© Sunshine of Happiness
BY SANDEEP RAVIDUTT SHARMA

We keep changing our views. When someone gives you a flower bouquet, you feel on the top of the world. Freshness of the flowers becomes your voice. Just after few days you feel liking throwing away the same flowers and your voice becomes screeching sound. Good or bad moments are temporary. Love each moment whether in favour or out of favour. LIVE NOW.

Don't risk your life unless you are set out to save many lives.

If you wanted to know how God looks like. All you have to do is the look into the eyes of a child.

© Sunshine of Happiness
BY SANDEEP RAVIDUTT SHARMA

Taking a dip into the holy river makes you sacred only when purity of thoughts prevails and is devoted to the Lord.

Always welcome Criticism made with a noble intention to push you towards perfection. Critics with negative intentions anyway will get buried under the layer of passed time and become history.

© **Sunshine of Happiness**
BY SANDEEP RAVIDUTT SHARMA

Trees appear to be dancing in the wind and enjoying the moment. This is possible only when they remain grounded. Uprooted tree has got no option but to lay dead. Always remain grounded even when you keep flying.

Life teaches you every minute. Thanks to the life lessons that you could come so far with confidence and hope.

© Sunshine of Happiness
BY SANDEEP RAVIDUTT SHARMA

Facing challenges in life while staying positive takes you to the door of success.

It hardly costs anything to smile. But when you smile, it is invaluable so Keep Smiling:)

When even after trying you can't become what others want you to be. Focus on what you want to be in life and make efforts to achieve it.

© **Sunshine of Happiness**
BY SANDEEP RAVIDUTT SHARMA

Don't get disturbed if the green leaves turn black. Tomorrow is another day. The sun shine has the power to convert the leaves back to green.

Problems die down soon if your focus is on developing solution.

© **Sunshine of Happiness**
BY SANDEEP RAVIDUTT SHARMA

Not everyone can crack jokes but laughter doesn't have any such limitations. Laugh and be happy.

Value of experience gained multiplies when it's shared.

Take it easy. It's your life and not a scientific calculation.

Those are exceptional ones who give orders in a request tone and still make the person feel and realise the task ownership.

Many a times we are not ready to change our perspective and starts believing whatever we see is the whole truth. Shedding our ego can help us in understanding each other's view and harmony would prevail.

The successful person knows the true value of efforts.

© Sunshine of Happiness
BY SANDEEP RAVIDUTT SHARMA

Letter to Dear Life...Dear Life Unveil the surprises of today. I'm eager to receive challenges so that using my skills, I can convert them into opportunities at the earliest. Yours truly....

Focus on attracting desires which not only benefits you but at the same time doesn't hurt anyone else.

Wishes and blessings benefit those who care for the mankind.

Value your freedom more than the money offered.

Remove Goggles of ego to see positivity all around.

Life pose challenges every minute. Don't just look at them but prepare yourself and fight out those challenges.

Don't gamble with your life and stay away from the path of dishonesty, greed, immorality, isolation and selfishness. Do invest in education, character building, simplicity and kindness.

Flowers fill up positivity all around. Just look at them, and you are sure to Smile.

Follow discipline in life to ensure growth.

Value those who believe in you and keep motivating whether It's Sun rise or Sun set.

Dark clouds try to cover the Sun but can't hide it for long.

Face the difficulties head on, and you unfold the hidden opportunities.

Celebrate each moment instead of making plans for a grand Celebration.

© **Sunshine of Happiness**
BY SANDEEP RAVIDUTT SHARMA

Flowers bloom and smile at you. Return the smile with a pleasant look and smile.

© **Sunshine of Happiness**
BY SANDEEP RAVIDUTT SHARMA

Slow down a bit and see the beautiful world around you. Sometimes forget to wear your watch around your mind. It would change your outlook towards life.

When someone tries to hang Truth, the noose loses its grip.

© **Sunshine of Happiness**
BY SANDEEP RAVIDUTT SHARMA

When someone hurts you or causes any kind of loss. You feel like taking revenge. It's a natural emotion. Action of revenge doesn't necessarily end in one go, it may become a chain of events. Sometimes you become the perpetrator and other times seen as a victim. Try to forgive in the first place itself.

Don't remain hostage to negative thoughts. Break free immediately by holding on to the power of Gratitude. Thank Mother Nature and divine presence of the Sky, Sun, Moon and the Stars that always assure you of not being left alone.

Those who cancel lot of things planned earlier are the ones looking for excuses when they fail.

Winners prefer to walk the talk.

Mistakes committed are the best teachers.

Good deeds don't need any recommendations.

Caring for each other makes the journey of life interesting.

© **Sunshine of Happiness**
BY SANDEEP RAVIDUTT SHARMA

Don't worry about what will happen tomorrow. Focus on today, tomorrow will be always in your favour.

Release your tensions and you start winning.

The mirror always tells you the truth. You can't pretend before the mirror.

© **Sunshine of Happiness**
BY SANDEEP RAVIDUTT SHARMA

Don't repent for name sake if you plan to repeat the same steps again.

© **Sunshine of Happiness**
BY SANDEEP RAVIDUTT SHARMA

If your mind continuously wanders then calm it with soothing music.

Excuse and Blame are the twin brothers residing in the mind of an incompetent person who likes failure. Success like stinted efforts.

Sunshine of Happiness
BY SANDEEP RAVIDUTT SHARMA

Deeds inspire more than the words. Look out for real-life achievers to draw inspiration.

Not everyone can digest the truth. Be ready to face the truth.

Don't gamble even if you hardly have anything to lose. Never lose your innocence, character and the will power to succeed through the righteous path.

© **Sunshine of Happiness**
BY SANDEEP RAVIDUTT SHARMA

Don't bother about what you have lost. Be thankful to the Lord for what you have gained.

Face the world with a smile, and the World is all yours.

Fly if you can in your thoughts and dreams.

Debate becomes a war when ego rules.

© **Sunshine of Happiness**
BY SANDEEP RAVIDUTT SHARMA

When you try, people may laugh at you... You should thank them for at least paying attention to you. Those who don't try are dead as stone.

It is not important about what you have been in the past. What you do today counts more.

© **Sunshine of Happiness**
BY SANDEEP RAVIDUTT SHARMA

Dark clouds may threaten your existence by shouting loud. Remember it's just a matter of time. The Golden Sun is on its way to confirm your hope and erase all kinds of dark traces.

Take things in the lighter vein and grasp whatever suits you.

Millions await Lord's blessings but few of them actually make efforts to receive it in time.

© Sunshine of Happiness
BY SANDEEP RAVIDUTT SHARMA

Not everyone knows the importance of finding happiness in small things which culminates into an Ocean of joy.

Wish others by words spoken from your heart.

Always remember those who reside in the tallest towers are not aliens but human like you. Keep this basic principle in mind and you no longer feel inferior or superior when it's time to communicate.

Fly free with no baggage of the past.

© **Sunshine of Happiness**
BY SANDEEP RAVIDUTT SHARMA

If your view gets blocked due to any reason. Don't make attempt to remove the blockade, change your position and go for a slightly different view. Be the change instead of changing everything else.

Use your wit to diffuse tension among your peers.

Declare your good intentions before hand. It helps others to decide whether or not to support you in your endeavor.

© **Sunshine of Happiness**
BY SANDEEP RAVIDUTT SHARMA

Perspective changes with the person. Each of us sees and lives life with a fresh perspective. Sometimes when the view is blurred out, there is nothing wrong in understanding and using someone else's perspective and see the full picture.

© Sunshine of Happiness
BY SANDEEP RAVIDUTT SHARMA

If nothing works in your life, don't worry to relax for a while. Things will be alright.

Don't run away from problems in life. Stop, understand, plan and break it with simplicity.

Don't hesitate to try again if you have failed earlier.

Don't repent forever for actions taken in the past as no one really knows the after effects of your present action in the future.

© Sunshine of Happiness
BY SANDEEP RAVIDUTT SHARMA

Don't leave anything for tomorrow.

Tomorrow is another day. Things will change for better. Hope never dies.

Those who don't like to wait sometimes misses out a golden opportunity by a second.

Tone down if you have realised your mistake.

© **Sunshine of Happiness**
BY SANDEEP RAVIDUTT SHARMA

The universe delivers only when you ask for it.

© **Sunshine of Happiness**
BY SANDEEP RAVIDUTT SHARMA

Sometimes your existing knowledge also stops you to adopt fresh perspective towards life.

Don't give up...try your best... you can still achieve your aim. If needed give up your mistrust, unkind behaviour, arrogance, material pursuit and ill feelings towards others.

© **Sunshine of Happiness**
BY SANDEEP RAVIDUTT SHARMA

Plant trees of happiness in your mind through positive thoughts.

www.ingramcontent.com/pod-product-compliance
Lightning Source LLC
Chambersburg PA
CBHW031440210526
45464CB00005B/2275